We Are Here

Written by Scott Weiss

Illustrated by Katie Williams

We are here.

We are here,
because having a play partner
feels good.

We are here,
because everyone needs a cuddle.

We are here,
because we know sharing is the best.

We are here,
because being silly is serious business.

We are here, even when there is a loss.

We are here,
because surprises come in all shapes.

We are here, because it's fun to play in the water.

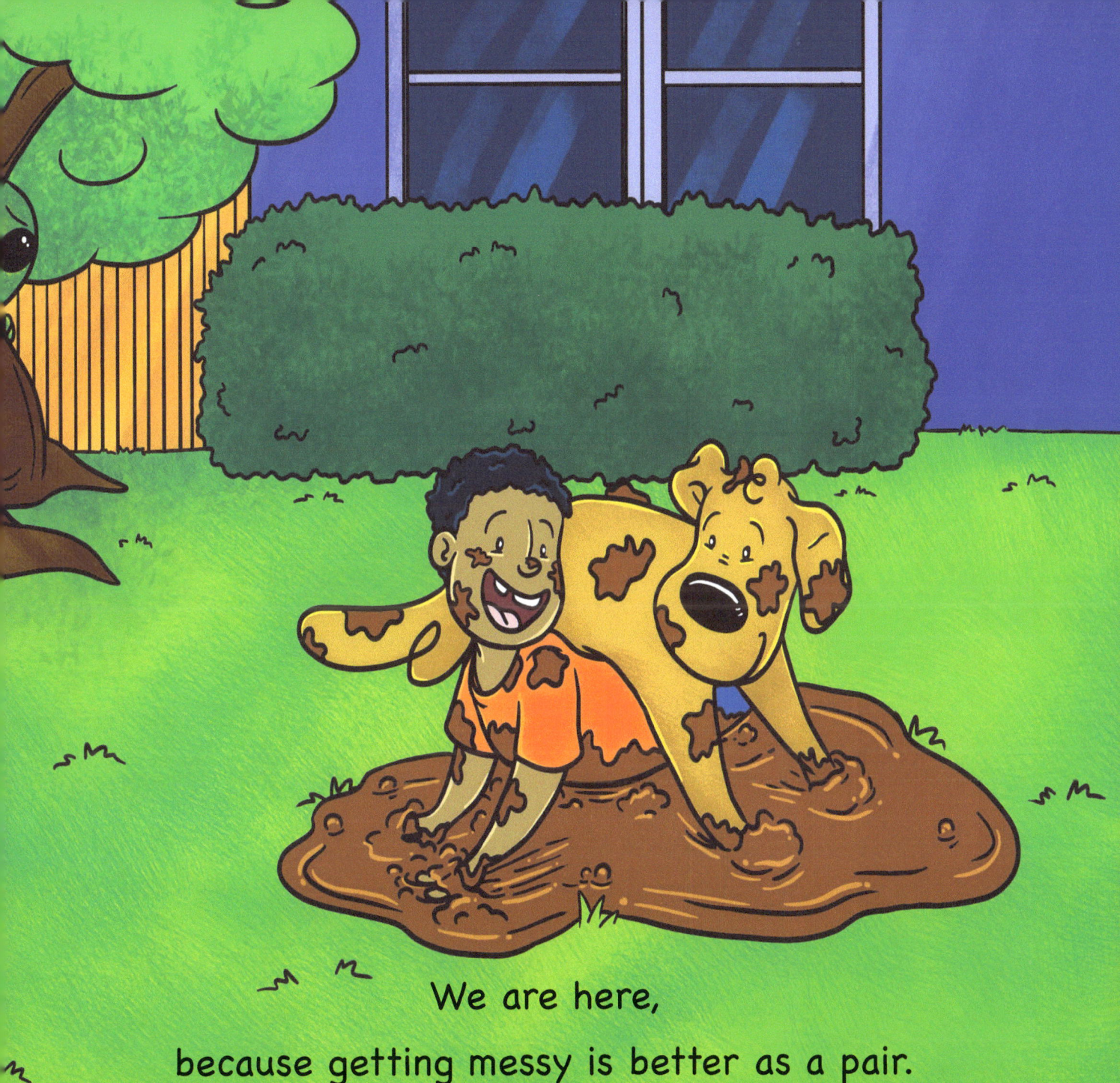

We are here,
because getting messy is better as a pair.

We are here,
because thunderstorms can be scary.

We are here,
because birthdays are awesome.

We are here, because arguments do happen.

We are here,
because it takes courage
to try.

We are here,
because it's okay to try again.

We are here,
even when you can't sleep at night.

We are here for your first day of school.

We are here for your last.

We are here,
because we all need an audience.

We are here, especially in town.

We are here,
in fact... We are up here, too.

We are here,
because we don't look scary.

We are here, because we love to share.

We are here, because this world is beautiful.

We are here,
because no one needs
to feel alone.

We are here,
because we want
everyone to feel loved.

We are here,
and we thank you for the love you share with us.

We are here.

About the Author

Scott Weiss is a first-time author who set out to honor the passing of his wife, Jenny, and their beloved golden retriever, Shammy. **We Are Here** is his tribute to them.

An enthusiastic father to his 13-year-old daughter Sam and 16-year-old son Tanner, Scott and his children live in Boulder, Colorado. Originally from Long Island, NY, Scott is an adrenaline-seeker who enjoys skiing and mountain biking in the Rocky Mountains surrounding Boulder.

Dedicated to

Jenny Primak Weiss - 1972-2015
and Shammy Sierra Weiss - 1999-2012

Many minds touch a book in the process of its writing. The elements of **We Are Here** were part of an imagined story that I shared with Jenny, which centered around how much love our golden retriever Shammy had given to us through her life.

After Jenny passed away in 2015, I thought a lot about how to honor her life while staying true to myself in the process. Jenny thrived in her days spent as an elementary school teacher, so creating a children's book based upon this imagined story seemed the perfect tribute.

We Are Here isn't just my story; it's our story. It gives the young reader a glimpse into the day-to-day experiences of how children bond with their dogs and then surprises them with an otherworldly twist.

Copyright ©2022 Scott Weiss/We Are Here, LLC

ALL RIGHTS RESERVED.

No part of this publication may be reproduced, stored in a retrieval system, or transmitted in any form or by any means — electronic, mechanical, photocopy, recording, or any other — except for brief quotation in reviews, without the prior permission of the author or publisher.

ISBN: 978-0-578-25907-9 (hardcover)
978-0-578-25908-6 (paperback)

Creative Director: Joanne Boufis
Creative Team: Paige DeBoer
Illustrator: Katie Williams

Published by JoFactor Entertainment, LLC
www.JoFactor.com

CPSIA information can be obtained
at www.ICGtesting.com
Printed in the USA
BVHW020946240522
637935BV00009B/515